Illustrated
STORIES from the
BOOK of MORMON

Illustrated STORIES *from the* BOOK *of* MORMON

Volume: 3

Raymond H. Jacobs, *Artist*

Dr. Clinton F. Larson, *Narrative and Editing*
Professor of English, Brigham Young University

Joseph N. Revill, *Correlator and Writer*

Published by
PROMISED LAND PUBLICATIONS, INC.
Salt Lake City, Utah

FIRST EDITION VOLUME 3 1968

Lithographed in U.S.A.
PROMISED LAND PRESS
Salt Lake City, Utah

Contents

Foreword. 4

Acknowledgments. 9

Portraits in Words 7

Maps of Possible Routes of Nephite Journey 8-9

A Short History of the Church of Jesus Christ of
  Latter-day Saints (Chap. 3) with Illustrations 10-14

  Joseph Smith as a young man 10

  The Three Witnesses of the Plates of the Book
    of Mormon 11

  Melchizedek Priesthood Restored. 12

  Eight Witnesses of the Plates of the Book of
    Mormon 13

  The Book of Mormon is Published. 13

  Church of Jesus Christ of Latter-day Saints is
    Organized 14

Moroni's Challenge. 16

Character page 17

Book of Mormon Illustrations with narrative
  by Dr. Clinton F. Larson 18-114

  Nephi's marriage. 18

  The Lord speaks to Lehi. 21

  Lehi discovers the Liahona 22

  Lehi and family begin their journey
    into the wilderness. 24

  Encampment at Shazer 26

  Nephi and brothers hunt game for food. 27

  Journey continues, following direction of
    the Liahona 28

  Nephi breaks his bow. 30

  Nephi's brothers complain of hardships 31

  Nephi makes a new bow 32

  Lehi and Nephi use the Liahona to find food. 33

  Nephi returns from successful hunt 34

  Journey continues to Nahom 35

  Death of Ishmael 36

  Ishmael's daughters complain to Lehi about their
    father's death. 38

  Laman and Lemuel plot against Lehi and Nephi 40

  The Lord speaks to Laman and Lemuel 41

  Journey continues into desert wilderness 42

  The families live on raw meat in wilderness. 44

  Jacob and Joseph are born during travels. 46

  Living in the wilderness 47

  Arrival in Bountiful by the Sea Irreantum 48

  The Lord appears to Nephi atop a mountain. 50

  Nephi finds ore for tools 51

  Nephi constructs bellows 52

  Tools made for construction of a ship 53

  Laman and Lemuel and Ishmael's sons mock Nephi. . . . 54

  Nephi's brothers argue with him 56

  Nephi instructs his brothers 57

  Nephi shocks his brothers through the power of
    the Lord. 59

Laman and Lemuel repent and worship the Lord. 61

The brothers construct a ship. 62

Nephi prays atop a mountain. 64

The Lord talks to Lehi 65

Lehi's company boards ship with supplies 66

Ship sails out to sea 68

The family begins to make merry. 70

Nephi is lashed to the mast by brothers. 72

Nephi is bound to the mast 73

The Liahona stops working 74

Ship wallows in a tempest 75

Nephi is finally freed 76

Lehi is stricken ill 78

Sariah and Nephi's wife are stricken ill 79

Nephi's brothers repent and seek Nephi's help. 80

The Promised Land is sighted. 81

The immigrants begin farming 82

Nephi and brothers explore wonders of the
  Promised Land. 84-85

Nephi makes plates of ore 86

Nephi engraves record of his father 87

Nephi explains to family about the record. 88

Nephi quotes the prophet Zenos. 90

Nephi reads from Brass Plates of Laban. 92

Nephi reads Isaiah's prophecies 94

Illustrations of Isaiah's prophecies 96-99

  Rulers of the Nations of the world will eventually
    acknowledge the Lord 96

  Prisoners of darkness to come into light. 98

  Israelites shall gather to safety 99

Nephi's brothers inquire as to the meaning of
  Isaiah's words 100

Nephi explains prophecies (following illustration) 101-107

  A mighty nation of Gentiles to be established. 102

  Jews to be scattered abroad after rejecting
    Christ 103

  The message on plates to come forth; Moroni to
    complete record and Joseph Smith to
    receive it. 104

  The Lord's covenants revealed. 105

  Israel in exodus from captivity 106

  Nations to war against Israel's gathering. 107

Nephi warns of destruction to come to the wicked 110

Nephi foretells coming of Christ. 112

False churches and doctrines to fall 113

Nephi testifies of truth on the Plates 114

Pearls for Thought
  by Alma E. Gygi 115

Book of Mormon text - 1 Nephi 16:7 through 22:31 116-126

Moroni's Challenge. 127

Appreciation to The First Presidency. 128

Preview of Volume 4 128

Foreword

"... the Lord giveth no commandments unto the children of men, save he shall prepare a way for them that they may accomplish the thing which he commandeth them."

1 Nephi 3:7

We rejoice with Nephi in the realization of God's promises as expressed above. Volume III of *Illustrated Stories from the Book of Mormon* affords us, and all readers of this record, a genuine exhibit of the fulfillment of these prophetic words.

When we contemplate the magnitude of the commandments given to Lehi and Nephi, we can but marvel at their accomplishments. With Lehi and Nephi we must acknowledge God's hand and direction in their achievement.

The task of illustrating this portion of Nephi's record presented some problems which need special mention.

We are aware of Nephi's expression concerning the ship which he built, that he worked the timbers not after the manner of men, but after the manner which God showed him. We realize that the design and structure of this vessel followed a blueprint furnished Nephi by the Lord. Unfortunately, Nephi did not pass on a copy of these plans. We were, therefore, obliged to improvise a design for this ship which in all likelihood has little resemblance to his ship. However, we could not merely leave a blank space in the illustration to accommodate the idea of a ship whose shape and detail we could not portray accurately. We know the ship had a mast, sails, upper and lower deck, bunks or beds, and a steering mechanism.

We beg your indulgence in accepting our humble efforts in these art pieces, to illustrate and interpret the events of Nephi's experiences as being authentic, only to the extent as available facts enable us correctly to portray them.

It is necessary at times to improvise a familiar scene to express the meaning or subject spoken centuries ago by God's prophets. Nephi in his record referred to Isaiah's writing found on the Brass Plates of Laban. Many of Isaiah's expressions refer to our very day, and we are presently witnessing their fulfillment.

Isaiah's expression, that the rulers of the nations of the world will eventually see and acknowledge Jesus Christ as the Savior of the world, presents a problem of illustration which requires some improvisation. We determined that we could best and most simply portray Isaiah's insight by using a familiar scene representing the rulers of the nations of the world. We do not intend here to convey a thought or belief that the Savior will appear to these rulers at the United Nations headquarters. This portrayal is purely figurative.

It is our hope and desire that the efforts we express here will encourage a complete study of the Book of Mormon. We acknowledge it to be the most nearly perfect book in the earth.

— *The Publishers*

Acknowledgments

Volume III of *Illustrated Stories from the Book of Mormon* has required a tremendous effort on the part of a great many people. We again acknowledge, with great appreciation, the efforts of our advisory board in making the interpretations portrayed in this volume. To Dr. Sidney B. Sperry, Dr. Ellis T. Rasmussen, Dr. Daniel H. Ludlow, Dr. Paul R. Cheesman, Dr. Ross T. Christensen, Dr. Clinton F. Larson, Golden Berrett, and Alma E. Gygi we express our thanks and appreciation for their help. To sit for hours in a story meeting with this group is an unforgettable experience. To see the results of their years of research and study climax in the expressions portrayed in these volumes, all brought together under the influence of the Holy Spirit, makes one thankful for the blessing of their association.

We are greatly indebted to Dr. Clinton F. Larson for his splendid creation of the story narrative which accompanies the illustrations. It is no small task to interpret prophetic writing and put them on an easily understandable plane for all ages. Dr. Larson has accomplished a great work in this, and we are appreciative of his fine talent.

Again we acknowledge the masterful touch of our art director, Mr. Raymond H. Jacobs, who so skillfully portrays the advisory board's interpretations. We acknowledge the efforts of Henry Helsloot, Stuart Heimdal, Max Mahan, and Judith Clarke, who have ably assisted Mr. Jacobs in these art expressions.

We are truly appreciative of the hundreds of letters we have received from our subscribers expressing their gratitude for our work.

It is gratifying to receive expressions such as one coming from a subscriber in Kaysville, Utah. This good woman gives credit to our publication as having brought a rich experience of spirituality into her family. Others have made similar expressions, all of which give us impetus and determination to complete our undertaking.

Space does not permit our detailing all of the wonderful expressions we have received and heard; so we take this opportunity of thanking everyone. We do, however, desire to here acknowledge one heart-touching experience which came to our attention recently. A young family at Spokane, Washington, having seen our publications, expressed a desire to acquire them at a later date. In the interim, tragedy and grief struck their lives. The young wife and mother of three small children was called in death. The young family called our sales representative and asked her to arrange for the subscription to *Illustrated Stories from the Book of Mormon* as a memorial to their wife and mother.

We feel highly honored that our publication merits in their eyes such an honored position. We extend to the Edward Siniff family, of Spokane, our heartfelt sympathy in their great loss. We hope our publications will help instill an abiding testimony in the truth of the gospel of Jesus Christ and the promises of eternal salvation for those who follow its direction.

The historic writing and the correlating material in this volume is from the pen of Joseph N. Revill, who acts as chairman of the advisory board.

— *The Publishers*

Portraits in Words

by Joseph N. Revill

For a number of years, there has been a great controversy about who should get credit for the discovery of America. My early history lessons fixed this honor on Christopher Columbus. He was, according to those same theorists, supposed to be disproving that the world was flat. These same advocates theorized that he was the first great mariner to sail out into the blue, unknown Atlantic.

I call these "theories" because recent facts of a sufficient number establish beyond question that a number of mariners touched the shores of North or South America many times before Columbus' venture.

Leif Ericson touched North America nearly five hundred years before Columbus. The extensive sailing of the seas was not an uncommon practice and did not originate with either of these adventurers.

I do not mean to take any glory or credit away from Columbus. He it was who informed the world in 1492 that America existed. In Volume II of this work, we portrayed Columbus as being among the Gentiles who were separated from the people of this land by many waters. Nephi records, ". . . the spirit of God that it came down and wrought upon the man; and he went forth upon the many waters, even unto the seed of my brethren, who were in the promised land." Nephi further records his father Lehi as saying, "It is wisdom that this land should be kept as yet from the knowledge of other nations . . ."

What of Columbus' history—was he prompted by the Spirit of God? To answer we quote from a biography *Columbus, Don Quixote of the Seas*, by Jacob Wasserman. On page 18 the author records that Columbus wrote:

> "From my first youth onward, I was a seaman, and have so continued until this day. Wherever ship has been I have been. I have spoken and treated with learned men, priests and layman, Latin and Greeks, Jews and Moors, and with many men of other faiths. The Lord was well disposed to my desire and he bestowed upon me courage and understanding; knowledge of seafaring he gave me in abundance; of astrology as much as was needed, and of geometry and astronomy likewise. Further, he gave me joy and cunning in drawing maps and thereon cities, mountains, rivers, islands and the harbors, each one in its place. I have seen and truly I have studied all books, cosmographies, histories, chronicles and philosophies, and other arts, for which our Lord with provident hand unlocked my mind, sent me upon the seas, and gave me fire for the deed. Those who heard of my emprise called it foolish, mocked me, and laughed. But who can doubt but that the Holy Ghost inspired me?" And to King Ferdinand, Columbus wrote, after his success, "I came to your majesty as the emissary of the Holy Ghost." (p. 46)

There can be little doubt that Columbus played his part in God's plan. He was sent forth when the Lord was ready to have the knowledge of this land known generally throughout the world. The Lord was ready to reveal the place where He had led many of His people, with some of whom He had made a covenant.

Writers of histories, encyclopedias, and scientific papers have contended for many years that the people who were on this land when Columbus arrived were descendants of those who had found their way across the ice of Bering Strait. They have discounted that any migration arrived here by sea before Columbus.

No doubt there were migrations by way of the Bering Strait; there can be no doubt also that there were numerous landings on this continent at various times from the sea. Why should it be thought by anyone to be incredible that men should find their way to this land over the sea?

Caspian
Sea

ASSYRIA

Mediterranean Sea

SIDON
TYRE
• NINEVEH

JUDAH
BABYLON •
JERUSALEM
BABYLONIA
• PERSOPOLIS

IDUMEA
1st. CAMP
PERSIA

Persian Gulf

Red Sea

ARABIA

EMPTY QUARTER

Quara Mts.

BOUNTIFUL

N
W E
S

Arabian Sea

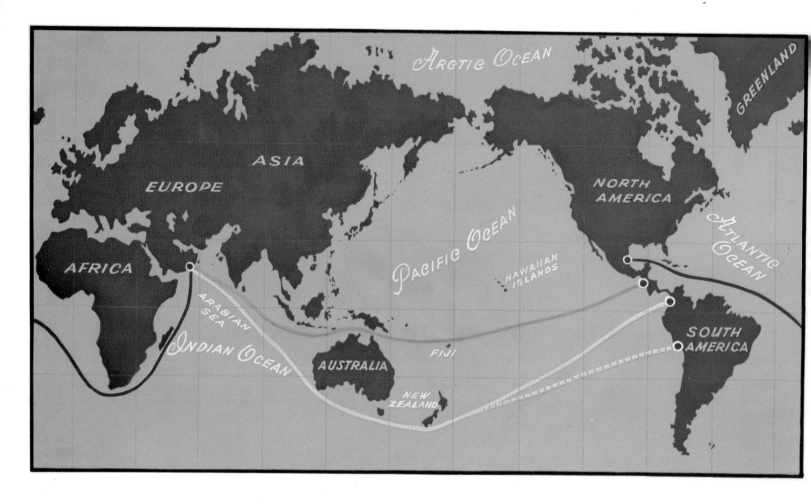

During the days of Solomon, his ships sailed through many seas and to many lands. The Phoenicians were noted for their explorations and world commerce which they conducted mostly by sea. Time may prove that the land Solomon knew as Ophir was in reality what we know as South America. The treasures and precious items he got from Ophir may have come from this continent of the new world.

It is now a well-established truth that other sea voyages similar to that of Lehi and his family occurred around the same time. From a Phoenician inscription found at Parahyba, Brazil, and now well authenticated, we learn:

> "We are Sons of Canaan from Sidon, the city of the king. Commerce has cast us on this distant shore, a land of Mountains. We set a youth for the exalted gods and goddesses in the nineteenth year of Hiram, our mighty king. We embarked from Ezion-Geber into the Red Sea and voyaged with ten ships. We were at sea together for two years around the land belonging to Ham but were separated by a storm and we were no longer with our companions. So we have come here, twelve men and three women on a . . . shore which I, The Admiral, control. But auspiciously may the exalted gods and goddesses favor us!"

We quote this from an article by Cyrus H. Gordon of Waltham, Massachusetts: "The authenticity of the Phoenician Text from Parahyba," published in *Pontificium Institutum Biblicum*, it is also printed in *Newsweek*, May 27, 1968, p. 62, and *Time Magazine*, May 24, 1968, p. 62.

For purposes of orientation only, we here publish two maps of the area involved in Lehi's journey. It is not our intent, and we do not desire, to affix the geography of this journey. There are a number of opinions as to the route and eventual landing spot of these Nephites. We shall leave this problem to the individual student and direct his study to numerous good texts: *An Introduction to the Study of the Book of Mormon*, by J. M. Sjodahl; *Ancient America and the Book of Mormon*, by Milton R. Hunter; *The Book of Mormon Compendium*, by Sidney B. Sperry.

Our testimony is that America is the Promised Land, a land of liberty to the righteous, that the Lord will protect those who keep His commandments, and that He will preserve this land unto them.

A Short History of The Church of Jesus Christ of Latter-day Saints

CHAPTER 3.

by Joseph N. Revill

It was now early June, 1829. Feelings were running high against the young prophet and his scribe, Oliver Cowdery. But in spite of this, Joseph continued the task of translating from the plates. At this time the family of Peter Whitmer, Sr., offered a refuge and protection to Joseph and his work. They therefore moved to the Whitmer home at Fayette, Seneca County, N. Y., where they were graciously provided with facilities and sustenance that the work could proceed unmolested to a speedy completion. Young David, John, and Peter Whitmer, Jr., became staunch friends to Joseph Smith. Soon David and Peter, Jr., together with Joseph's brother, Hyrum, were baptized, increasing the membership of the new movement to a total of six.

As the translation of the plates progressed, the promise that three special witnesses should see and testify to the authenticity of this work was made known to the translator. Immediately, Oliver Cowdery, David Whitmer, and Martin Harris expressed the desire that they be allowed to be these witnesses. They were so insistent that Joseph inquired of the Lord regarding this desire. He received a revelation through the Urim and Thummim, and it is now recorded in Section 17 of the Doctrine and Covenants.

Shortly after this commandment was received, the prophet, his wife, his father and mother, Oliver Cowdery, the entire Whitmer family, and Martin Harris observed their usual morning devotion at the Whitmer home. As they arose from their prayers, Joseph approached Martin Harris and said, "Martin Harris, you have got to humble yourself before your God this day, that you may obtain a forgiveness of your sins. If you do, it is the will of God that you should look upon the plates in company with Oliver Cowdery and David Whitmer."

The four thereupon retired into the wood near the Whitmer home and prayed solemnly to God that they be allowed to see the plates. Joseph was first to pray vocally; each of the others followed in turn. After two unsuccessful attempts to get an answer to their prayers, Martin suggested that he withdraw, as he felt his presence prevented their receiving the answer they sought.

After Martin had left, the trio again engaged in fervent prayer, and not many minutes passed when they observed a brilliant light above them in the air and an angel standing before them. The angel held the plates and turned the pages one by one that the viewers might see engravings on them. The angel then spoke; "David, blessed is the Lord, and he that keeps his commandments." Immediately they all heard a voice from out of the bright light above them, saying, "These plates have been revealed by the power of God, and they have been translated by the power of God. The translation of them which you have seen is correct, and I command you to bear record of what you now see and hear."

As the vision closed, the prophet Joseph went in search for Martin Harris, whom he found some distance into the woods fervently, but without success, calling on the Lord for an answer. Joseph joined Martin in prayer, and after considerable time and effort they received the same vision experienced by the three earlier. The experience caused Martin to exclaim, "'Tis enough; 'tis enough; mine eyes have beheld; mine eyes have beheld; Hosanna."

It must have been a source of great joy and comfort to Joseph Smith now to have some company in the important and unusual task entrusted to him.

He was now no longer alone in the knowledge and testimony of the angelic ministrations and the existence of the sacred plates.

In compliance with the commandment given them, Oliver Cowdery, David Whitmer, and Martin Harris gave documented testimony of their experience, which now appears in every copy of the Book of Mormon, as follows:

THE TESTIMONY OF THREE WITNESSES

Be it known unto all nations, kindred, tongues, and people, unto whom this work shall come: That we, through the grace of God the Father, and our Lord Jesus Christ, have seen the plates which contain this record, which is a record of the people of Nephi, and also of the Lamanites, their brethren, and also of the people of Jared, who came from the tower of which hath been spoken. And we also know that they have been translated by the gift and power of God, for his voice hath declared it unto us; wherefore we know of a surety that the work is true. And we also testify that we have seen the engravings which are upon the plates; and they have been shown unto us by the power of God, and not of man. And we declare with words of soberness, that an angel of God came down from heaven, and he brought and laid before our eyes, that we beheld and saw the plates, and the engravings thereon; and we know that it is by the grace of God the Father, and our Lord Jesus Christ, that we beheld and bear record that these things are true. And it is marvelous in our eyes. Nevertheless, the voice of the Lord commanded us that we should bear record of it; wherefore, to be obedient unto the commandments of God, we bear testimony of these things. And we know that if we are faithful in Christ, we shall rid our garments of the blood of all men, and be found spotless before the judgment-seat of Christ, and shall dwell with him eternally in the heavens. And the honor be to the Father, and to the Son, and to the Holy Ghost, which is one God.   Amen.

Oliver Cowdery
David Whitmer
Martin Harris

Now that the heavens were opened, young Joseph received an almost constant flow of information, instructions, and revelation, coupled with angelic visitation. Joseph Smith and Oliver Cowdery had received the Aaronic Priesthood, and John the Baptist at that time had promised them in due course that they would be given the Melchizedek Priesthood. Another angelic visitation of vast importance occurred sometime between May 15 and the end of June, 1829 (the exact date is unknown). This event took place in the woods between Harmony, Susquehanna County, Penn., and Colesville, Broome County, New York, on the banks of the Susquehanna River. Peter, James, and John appeared to Joseph Smith and Oliver Cowdery and conferred upon them, by the laying on of hands, the Melchizedek Priesthood. This power and authority would give them all the keys to organize

and govern God's kingdom on earth in the last days.

Several of the revelations received during this formative period, into the early part of 1830, gave instructions as to the organization and government of the Church, and these are found as Section 18 and 20 of the Doctrine and Covenants.

It was not long after the three witnesses had had their visitation from Moroni, the angelic messenger, that Joseph Smith, Jr., several of the Whitmer family, Hyrum Page, and Joseph's father and his brothers, Samuel and Hyrum, were together at the Smith home in Manchester. They had gone there for the purpose of arranging at Palmyra for the publication of the Book of Mormon. While at the Smith home, this group retired to the woods nearby and were shown the plates by the prophet himself. This is the joint testimony they gave of their experience:

TESTIMONY OF EIGHT WITNESSES

Be it known unto all nations, kindred, tongues, and people, unto whom this work shall come: That Joseph Smith, Jr., the translator of this work, has shown unto us the plates of which hath been spoken, which have the appearance of gold; and as many of the leaves as the said Smith has translated we did handle with our hands; and we also saw the engravings thereon, all of which has the appearance of ancient work, and of curious workmanship. And this we bear record with words of soberness, that the said Smith has shown unto us, for we have seen and hefted, and know of a surety that the said Smith has got the plates of which we have spoken. And we give our names unto the world, to witness unto the world that which we have seen. And we lie not, God bearing witness of it.

                    Christian Whitmer
                    Jacob Whitmer
                    Peter Whitmer, Jr.
                    John Whitmer
                    Hyrum Page
                    Joseph Smith, Sr.
                    Hyrum Smith
                    Samuel H. Smith

Now that the translation was nearing completion, and the date for the organization of the Church had been set by commandment from God, arrangements needed to be made for publication of the Book of Mormon. In early 1830 agreement was made with E. B. Grandin of Palmyra, New York, to print 5,000 copies of the book at a cost of $3,000. A copyright was obtained and the work began. In compliance with a revelation to Joseph Smith and directed to Martin Harris given in March, 1830, the funds necessary to secure the work were to be provided through mortgage arrangements on the Harris farm property.

The publication was not without incidents and problems, and enemies of the work made numerous efforts to thwart the publication or destroy it. They even tried to compromise the copyright and print the book in a changed condition and serialize it in a periodical of the time. Organized effort on the part of the residents of the area interfered with the publication of the book, but precautions of all kinds were taken to insure its success. Oliver Cowdery made a second copy of the manuscript, and only one day's work at a time was delivered to the printer to avoid the possible chance of loss. Success was finally achieved.

On Tuesday, April 6, 1830, in compliance with the commandment given earlier by revelation, Joseph Smith, Jr., Oliver Cowdery, Hyrum Smith, Peter Whitmer, Jr., Samuel H. Smith, and David Whitmer assembled at the home of Peter Whitmer, Sr., and there proceeded to organize the Church of Jesus Christ of Latter-day Saints.

Now the little Church began officially to function, and Joseph Smith, Jr., was sustained as Prophet, Seer, and Revelator to the Church. This date saw others added to the membership rolls, among them the prophet's mother and father, and Martin Harris and Orrin Porter Rockwell.

On the Sabbath following the organization, which was April 11, 1830, Oliver Cowdery preached the first public discourse of the new Church. This date saw the baptism of Hyrum Page, his wife Katherine, Christian, Anne, Jacob, and Elizabeth Whitmer. The following week the Church membership rolls were enlarged by the baptism of Peter Whitmer, Sr., and his wife Mary, William, Elizabeth, and Vincent Jolly, Richard B. Peterson, and Elizabeth Anne Whitmer.

By June 9, 1830, when the first conference of the Church was held, the membership had increased to thirty, and included Newell Knight, who would play a prominent role in the Church during his lifetime. Thus the little Church began its career to spread doctrines of salvation abroad in the world, in the face of opposition and persecution, which seemed to ever increase.

I, Nephi, and my brothers fell in love with the daughters of Ishmael because they were beautiful in spirit and in appearance. I took one to wife, as did each of my brothers. Zoram took the eldest. The marriages were performed according to the will of the Lord. To show our love of the Lord, we consecrated ourselves to fulfill his commandments in righteousness.

See 1 Nephi 16:7

IN this way my father, Lehi, fulfilled all the commandments of the Lord which had been given to him, and so he was filled with great joy. I myself had been especially blessed. Later, the voice of the Lord spoke to my father by night and commanded him that he should begin his journey into the wilderness the next day.

See 1 Nephi 16:8-9

MY father arose the next morning and went to the door of the tent. He was amazed to find there on the ground a round ball of fine brass that was beautiful and strangely made. Within the ball were two spindles, and one of them pointed where we should go in the wilderness.

See 1 Nephi 16:10

WE gathered together everything we needed for our journey, and all that was left of our provisions that the Lord had given to us. We also took seeds of every kind that we might carry into the wilderness, across the river Laman. The land about us abounded with doves, goats, fowl, gazelles, and bees, and we were sorry that we had to leave it.

See 1 Nephi 16:11-12

WE travelled for four days in a south-southeast direction. Then we pitched our tents in a place that we called Shazer.

See 1 Nephi 16:13

WHEN we were settled, we went with our bows and arrows into the wilderness to slay food for our families. When we had enough, we returned to them at Shazer.

Then we continued our journey, in the same direction, keeping in the most fertile parts of the wilderness, which were in the borders near the Red Sea.

See 1 Nephi 16:14

E travelled for many days, slaying food, as we needed it, with our bows and arrows and our stones and slings. We kept looking into the brass ball to watch the spindle. It guided us into the most fertile parts of the wilderness.

My father, Lehi, held the ball very carefully, for he knew that it was the Lord's will that we should have it.

We travelled for many days, then stopped to rest and get food.

See 1 Nephi 16:15-17

ONE day, when I was out hunting, I broke my bow, which was made of fine steel. My brothers became angry with me because its loss meant that we could no longer get any food. We returned to our families empty handed, and because they were very tired from journeying they suffered all the more from their hunger.

See 1 Nephi 16:18-19

LAMAN and Lemuel and the sons of Ishmael began to murmur angrily because of our troubles and suffering in the wilderness. Even my father, Lehi, began to murmur against the Lord, asking why, if our people were doing the will of the Lord, we were encountering such hardship. Then everyone began to murmur against the Lord.

Not only was my bow broken, but my brothers' bows had lost their spring. It therefore became impossible for us to get any food.

But I talked to my brethren for a long time because they had hardened their hearts again and because they complained against the Lord their God.

See 1 Nephi 16:20-22

I Nephi, found a good piece of wood and made a bow out of it, and then I found a straight stick and made an arrow. I armed myself with my new bow and arrow, and with a sling and some stones. Then I asked my father where I should go to find some food.

My father prayed to the Lord for an answer because our family had humbled themselves after they heard me plead with them to soften their hearts and accept the Lord's will. I had pleaded with them and testified to them with the energy of my soul.

See 1 Nephi 16:23-24

THE voice of the Lord came to my father, and he was truly chastened because he had murmured against the Lord; then he became very sorry.

The voice then said, "Look at the ball, and read what is written there." My father did so; then he began to tremble in fear. My brothers and the sons of Ishmael and our wives saw him and also began to tremble.

Then I, Nephi, saw the pointers in the ball, and I too saw that they worked according to the faith and diligence and attention which we gave them.

There was some writing on them which was easy to read; it enabled us to understand the ways of the Lord. Every so often it was written and changed, according, always, to the faith and diligence we would accord it. We saw that the Lord might use small means to bring about great things.

See 1 Nephi 16:25-29

I went to the top of the mountain, according to the directions on the ball. There I slew wild beasts to get food for our families. When I returned to our tents with them, everyone was filled with joy to see the food I had brought. Our families humbled themselves in gratitude before the Lord and thanked him.

See 1 Nephi 16:30-32

WE began travelling again, nearly on the same course as in the beginning. After many days we pitched our tents again.

See 1 Nephi 16:33

OUR joy ended when Ishmael died. In our sorrow we prayed for the peace of his soul. To show our sorrow, we covered ourselves with sackcloth and ashes. We dressed Ishmael's body in robes of white and buried him in the place which was called Nahom.

See 1 Nephi 16:34

THE daughters of Ishmael were overcome with grief that Ishmael had died and that they suffered the hardships of travelling in the wilderness. They blamed my father, Lehi, because he had brought them out of the land of Jerusalem. They cried, "Our father is dead, we have gone without food and water, we have become tired and sick on this long journey, and we are afraid that we too will die in the wilderness." They also began murmuring against me and said that they wanted to return to Jerusalem.

See 1 Nephi 16:35-36

ONCE again Laman became rebellious. To Lemuel and the sons of Ishmael he said, "Let us kill Lehi, our father, and also our brother Nephi, who has raised himself up to be our ruler and our teacher, for we are his older brothers. He says that the Lord has talked with him and that angels have ministered to him! Anyone can see that he is lying! He tells us these things so that he can lead us away into a strange wilderness and rule over us, which is against the custom, and do with us what pleases him!" Lemuel and the sons of Ishmael believed him and became very angry.

See 1 Nephi 16:37-38

BUT the voice of the Lord came to them in a pillar of light and spoke to them at length, chastening them for their anger, suspicion, and rebelliousness. Afterwards, they forgot their anger and repented; so the Lord blessed us again with food, and we did not die.

See 1 Nephi 16:39

E continued our journey, but from that time on, to the east. The hardships and difficulties were great, and our wives bore children in the wilderness.

See 1 Nephi 17:1

OUR families lived on raw meat, for we could not build fires for the risk of being seen by bands of robbers. But we thrived and grew strong because of our hardships, and our wives found it easy to nurse their children, who, after a time, became almost as strong as men. The spiritual and physical strength of our families enabled them to travel in the wilderness without complaining.

44

See 1 Nephi 17:2

JACOB and Joseph were born during this time, and our number was increasing markedly.

See 1 Nephi 17:2

THE journey in the wilderness proved to us that the commandments of God must be fulfilled. We learned that if the children of men keep his commandments he will feed them and strengthen them in mind and body, and will provide the means to accomplish whatever he commands them to do. Because we obeyed him, we survived in the wilderness for eight years before we came to a land that we called Bountiful.

See 1 Nephi 17:3-4

47

BOUNTIFUL was a beautiful land because of its variety and the abundance of its fruit; there was also much wild honey. The vegetation was lush, and round about there were trees and mountains. The Lord had prepared this land for us. And then we saw the sea, which we called Irreantum, which means "many waters." In it, we could catch plenty of fish.

48

See 1 Nephi 17:5

WE pitched our tents by the seashore, and, although our hardships in the wilderness had been severe, we began to forget about them because in this land we called Bountiful we were surrounded by natural beauty and plentiful food. Though our possessions were simple, they helped sustain us; we slept on mattresses filled with reeds and kept water in bottles we had made on our journey.

49

See 1 Nephi 17:6

AFTER I, Nephi, had been in Bountiful for many days, the voice of the Lord came to me, saying, "Arise, and climb the mountain." So I arose and did as the voice directed. I prayed, and then the Lord spoke to me. He said that I should build a ship according to a design that he would show me. And then he said that it would be the way we would be taken across the sea to the promised land!

See 1 Nephi 17:7-8

I asked the Lord where I should go to find ore to melt so that I could make tools to build the ship according to his design. Then the Lord told me where to go to find it. Some of the tools I needed were a bellows to make steel from iron ore, a mattock, an adze, a saw, and a plane.

See 1 Nephi 17:9-10

ND so it was that from the skins of animals I made a bellows to blow a fire to a high temperature. Then I built the fire—the first big one we had had in years—by striking two stones together to get sparks. While we were in the wilderness we did not have to cook our food because the Lord had made it easy to eat, and sweet. The Lord was also our light in the wilderness, for we knew that he prepares a way for us if we keep his commandments, and we knew that this is also the way we might reach the promised land. The Lord told me that as we travelled we would know that he leads us and that he, the Lord, is God, and that he delivered us from destruction, out of the land of Jerusalem.

See 1 Nephi 17:11-14

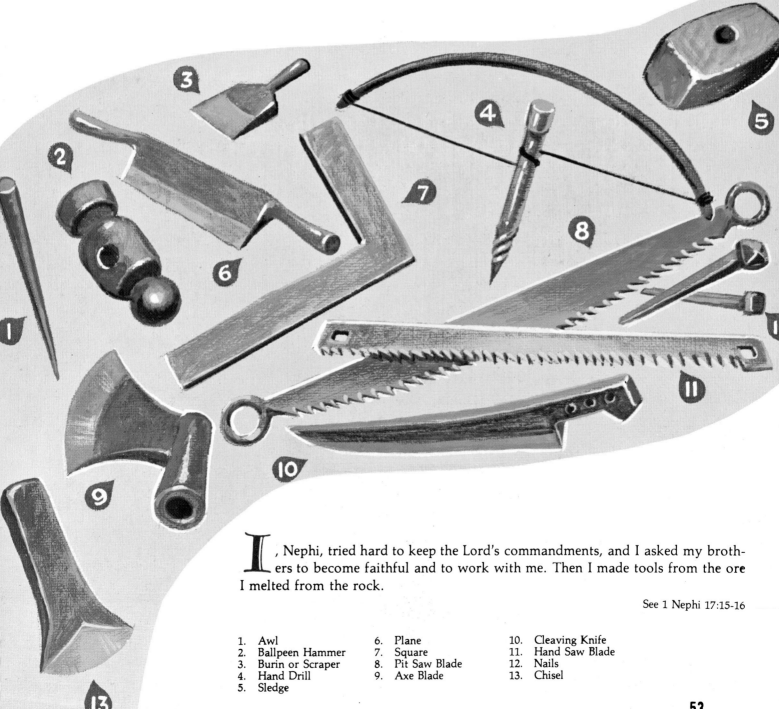

I, Nephi, tried hard to keep the Lord's commandments, and I asked my brothers to become faithful and to work with me. Then I made tools from the ore I melted from the rock.

See 1 Nephi 17:15-16

1. Awl
2. Ballpeen Hammer
3. Burin or Scraper
4. Hand Drill
5. Sledge
6. Plane
7. Square
8. Pit Saw Blade
9. Axe Blade
10. Cleaving Knife
11. Hand Saw Blade
12. Nails
13. Chisel

WHEN my brothers saw that I was getting ready to build a ship, they began to murmur against me. They said, "Our brother is a fool because he thinks that he can build a ship and cross the sea in it!" And so they complained against me and would not help me because they thought that I would fail. They would not believe that the Lord was telling me what to do and that I was obeying his commandments.

See 1 Nephi 17:17-18

I, Nephi, was sad because they had hardened their hearts, and when they saw me they became happy that I was sad. They said, "We knew that you could not build a ship because you do not have the judgment to complete such a great work. You are much like our father, Lehi. You are carried away by the foolish imagination of your heart, just as Lehi was as he led us in the wilderness, away from the land of Jerusalem. Our women have had to work while bearing children, and children have been born to them in the wilderness. Our women nearly died in their suffering. It would have been better for them if they had died before they left Jerusalem than for them to have suffered so much. All of us have been suffering in the wilderness while we might have been happy enjoying our possessions in the land of our inheritance. You know that the people of Jerusalem were righteous, for they obeyed the laws and judgments of the Lord, and all his commandments, according to the law of Moses. And we know that our father, Lehi, judged them falsely, and led us away simply because we listened to him. And you are just like him!"

See 1 Nephi 17:19-22

SO I, Nephi said to them, "Do you believe that our fathers, who were the children of Israel, would have been led away from the bondage of the Egyptians if they had not listened to the words of the Lord? The Lord commanded Moses to lead them away because they were given tasks that caused them to suffer grievously. Moses was commanded to do a great work. When he spoke, the Red Sea divided so that the children of Israel passed through on dry land. But when the armies of the

Pharaoh tried to follow, they were drowned, and you know, too, that the children of Israel were fed manna in the wilderness and that when Moses smote the rock, water flowed from it to quench their thirst. And even though Moses was leading them, and the Lord their God, the Redeemer, went before them to lead them by day and to give them light at night, and to give them all they needed, they hardened their hearts and became so unreasonable that they reviled against Moses and God. The Lord so established his word among them that nothing was done except by it, and after they had crossed the river Jordan he helped them overcome and drive out their enemies, whose fathers had taken the lands that rightfully belonged to them. Do you suppose that these enemies were righteous? No. Do you suppose that our fathers were any better than they if they had been righteous? No. To God, all people are the same, except that he favors the righteous. But this people had rejected every word of God and deserved immediate punishment for their sins. God was angry with them and so cursed the land against them, and blessed it so that it became a land of promise for our fathers. God wants the earth to be inhabited and possessed by his children, but he will help only those who are righteous, and he will enable them to prosper in it. He loves those like Abraham, Isaac, and Jacob who honor him by honoring his covenants with them. The children of Israel, like you, hardened their hearts; so the Lord chastened and corrected them. He sent flying fiery serpents to bite them, and then he made it possible for them to be healed, but because the way was simple and easy, many perished in their obstinacy. Even though they hardened their hearts now and then, God led them into the land of promise. But since that time they have become so wicked that they are in danger of a destruction that will surely come. Only a few will be led away into captivity. That is why the Lord commanded my father to go into the wilderness. Not only that, the Jews threatened to kill him, even as you have threatened to kill him. You are like those Jews, because you are murderers in your hearts. You fall into sin easily, and forget the Lord your God, even though you have seen an angel, who appeared to you and spoke to you, whose voice you have heard now and again, who also speaks to you as the still small voice of your conscience. But you do not feel anything, not even his words, even when his voice is like thunder. You also know that by the power of his almighty word the Lord can bring an end to the world and change the face of the land. So why can you be hard in your hearts? My heart aches for you, and I despair that you will be cast away from the Lord forever. And you know that the spirit of God caused me to speak as I do, and to try to bring you to repentance."

See 1 Nephi 17:23-47

WHEN I, Nephi, spoke to my brothers this way, they were angry with me and wanted to throw me into the sea. They were about to seize me when I said, "In the name of the Almighty God, I command you not to touch me, for I am so filled with the power of God, that my body may be consumed. Anyone who touches me will wither like a dried reed, and will become as nothing before the power of God, for God shall strike him." Then I told them that they should no longer murmur against their father, Lehi, and that they should work willingly with me because God commanded me that I should build a ship. I told them that this work would be done because God would make it possible. Surely the building of a ship would be an easy matter for God.

See 1 Nephi 17:48-51

FOR many days my brothers were so confused and stunned that they could not argue with me or lay their hands on me. So powerful was the spirit of God that they were afraid that they would wither if they did. Then the Lord said to me, "Stretch out your hand now to your brothers. They will not wither, but I will shock them, and I will do this that they might know that I am the Lord their God." I did, and my brothers shook before me, according to the word of the Lord. Then they said, "We surely know now that the Lord is with you and that it is his power that shook us." Then they fell down before me and were about to worship me, but I told them not to worship me, but to worship the Lord and to honor their father and mother that they might live a long time in the promised land.

See 1 Nephi 17:52-55

THEN they worshiped the Lord, and went forth with me to do as God commanded. We shaped the wood with our tools to make a ship. When we needed knowledge to solve a problem, the Lord gave it to me, and now and again he showed me how to work the timbers properly.

See 1 Nephi 18:1

I, Nephi, did not work the timbers according to the knowledge of the ship-builders of the time, but only according to what the Lord showed me, for I had faith that the Lord would enable us to reach the promised land.

See 1 Nephi 18:2

I went up into the mountain often to pray to the Lord, and the Lord blessed me by showing me many great things.

See 1 Nephi 18:3

WHEN I had finished the ship according to the will of the Lord, my brothers saw that it was good and that the workmanship was very fine, which caused them to humble themselves before the Lord again. Then the voice of the Lord came to my father, Lehi, that we should arise and go down into the ship.

See 1 Nephi 18:4-5

THE next day, as the Lord had commanded us, we prepared all we needed, including much fruit and meat from the wilderness, and the honey that was so plentiful. Then we went down into the ship and loaded our seeds and everything we had brought with us. With our wives and children, we boarded the ship and got ready to sail across the sea.

67

See 1 Nephi 18:6

OUR family now included my two new brothers; the older was called Jacob and the younger Joseph. Because our family was large and because we had prepared so carefully, we were very excited. We launched the ship and began to be driven before the wind toward the promised land.

See 1 Nephi 18:7-8

THE wind drove our ship for many days, far upon the sea. My brothers and the sons of Ishmael and their wives too began to make merry; they danced and sang and began to speak rudely, until they forgot that it was the power of the Lord that was carrying us across the sea.

See 1 Nephi 18:9

I, Nephi, was afraid that the Lord would get angry with us and smite us because we were sinful. Perhaps he would even let us be swallowed up in the depths of the sea! So I decided to talk to them to let them know again that, for our safety, they should obey the commandments of the Lord. But they became angry with me and told me that they would not let their younger brother rule them. Laman and Lemuel bound me with cords and punished me; but I knew that the Lord would show his power against their wickedness, according to his word.

See 1 Nephi 18:10-11

I was bound so tightly that I could not move.
See 1 Nephi 18:12-13

SUDDENLY, the compass stopped working! Then a storm raged around us for four days.

See 1 Nephi 18:12-13

WE were about to sink and drown. After we had been driven back for four days, my brothers saw that the judgment of God was upon them and that they would have to repent or die.

See 1 Nephi 18:15-16

SO they loosed the bands around my wrists and ankles, which had become very swollen and sore. But I did not complain about my troubles. Instead, I praised God for a whole day.

See 1 Nephi 18:15-16

MY father, Lehi, talked to my brothers and the sons of Ishmael, but they threatened him for defending me. He had become sad because of the troubles of his children and their sins, and because he and Sariah were old they became very sick and almost died.

See 1 Nephi 18:16

THEN Jacob and Joseph became grieved because their mother was stricken. My wife and children wept, and pleaded with my brothers to release me. But in their anger against me they swore that they would not.

See 1 Nephi 18:17-19

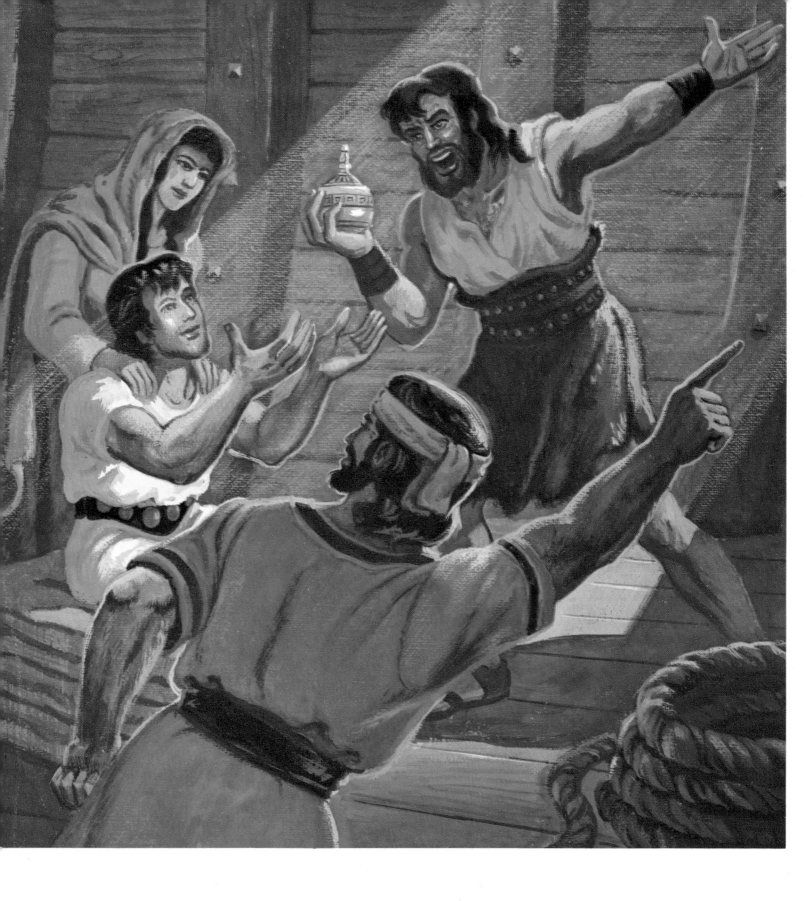

NOTHING but the power of the Lord, which had caused the storm, could soften the hearts of my brothers. Then the storm released its fury, and the wind beat against our ship and the waves crested over it. Just as we were about to sink into the depths of the sea, my brothers repented and freed me.

See 1 Nephi 18:20

A S soon as they let me go, I took the compass, and it worked in the direction and way I wanted it to work. Then I prayed to the Lord. Very soon the winds died down and the storm stopped, and a great calm came upon the sea. I guided the ship for a time, and then in the distance we sighted the promised land! We landed, quickly pitched our tents, and called the land by those words—the promised land.

See 1 Nephi 18:21-23

E began to till the earth and plant the seeds that we had brought from Jerusalem. Soon we had wonderful and abundant crops.

See 1 Nephi 18:24

E travelled many places in the wilderness of the promised land, and we found beasts of the forest of every kind, and the cow and the ox, and the donkey and the horse, the goat and the wild goat, and all kinds of animals which are for the use of man. We also found all kinds of ore, both of gold and silver, and of copper.

See 1 Nephi 18:25

THE Lord commanded me to make plates from the ore we had found, that I might engrave on them the records of my people. This I did, and I engraved the record of my father, of our journeying in the wilderness, and of the prophecies of my father; then I engraved a record of my own prophecies.

See 1 Nephi 19:1

WHEN I made these first plates, I did not know that the Lord would command me to make another set of plates. I engraved on the first plates the record of my father, the genealogy of his father, and the greater part of all our adventures in the wilderness. What happened before I made these small plates is engraved in more detail on the first plates. After I made the small plates, the Lord commanded me that I should engrave on them a record of the more plain and precious parts of the ministry and the prophecies, and that these should be kept for the instruction of my people, who should possess the land, and for other wise purposes that are known to the Lord.

See 1 Nephi 19:2-10

THE first plates also contain a greater account of the wars and contentions and destructions of my people. I commanded my people what they should do after I am gone, that these plates should be handed down from one generation to another, or from one prophet to another, until further commandments were given from the Lord. An account of the making of these plates will be given hereafter, but I continue my work of recording the sacred things that are to be kept for the knowledge of my people. And I testify that according to the words of the angel the Lord will come in six hundred years from the time my father left Jerusalem. Men will consider these records in the same way that they consider the Lord when he shall come — as nothing.

They will scourge and smite the Lord, and he will endure the pain; they will spit on him because of his loving kindness and his long suffering toward them. The Lord will be lifted up and crucified for them, then buried in a sepulchre. The three days of darkness that will come on the earth will be a sign to those who live on the islands of the sea, but more especially to those who are of the house of Israel. The angel told me that the story of the sacrifice of the Lord will be according to the words of the prophets Zenock, Neum, and Zenos of the Hebrew people—the same Lord who led our fathers out of bondage in Egypt and preserved them, the God of Abraham, Isaac, and Jacob of old.

See 1 Nephi 19:2-10

THE prophecy of Zenos was that the Lord, shortly after his crucifixion, would visit all the house of Israel. Some will hear his voice, because of their righteousness, to their great joy and salvation, but others will see only the thunderings and lightnings of his power, by the tempest, the fire, smoke, the vapor of darkness, the openings of the earth from earthquakes, and the mountains that will be thrown up from the violence under them. The rocks of the earth will be torn open, and the face of the land will change. The spirit of God will come upon the kings of the isles of the sea as they witness these things, and they will cry, "The God of nature suffers!" Those in Jerusalem who will crucify

the Lord will turn their hearts from him and reject his signs and wonders and the power and glory of the God of Israel. Because they will despise the Lord, they will wander over the land and become a hiss and a by-word, and the nations will hate them. But according to the prophecy of this same Zenos these people will finally accept the Lord as the Holy One of Israel; then they will remember the covenants that he made with their fathers. Then the Lord will remember the people of the islands of the sea and all the people of the house of Israel, and he will gather the house of Israel from the four quarters of the earth. All the earth will see that he is indeed the Lord, and every nation, kindred, tongue, and people shall be blessed.

See 1 Nephi 19:11-17

I, Nephi, have written these things to my people and to all the house of Israel to persuade them to remember the Lord their Redeemer. My spirit has worked so mightily with these truths that I am weary and weak and heavy of heart for those of Jerusalem. But the Lord has been merciful to me to show me these things; otherwise, I would have perished. I have been blessed by the same knowledge that was given to the prophets of old.

I taught my brothers about the prophecies, and the many things that were engraved on the plates of brass, so that they would know how the Lord deals with the children of men in other lands and times. I read to them from the book of Moses, but to persuade them more fully to believe in the Lord their Redeemer I read to them from the writings of Isaiah. The stories of the people in the scriptures are like our story, and I told my brothers to profit and learn from them. I said, "Listen to the prophet, for we are a branch of the house of Israel that has been broken off. Our hope lies in learning from the story of the house of Israel, that all might be saved."

See 1 Nephi 19:18-24

MOLECH, a God of the Ammonite nation, to whom the Ammonites sacrified children, Isaiah continually warned the Israelites not to be influenced by them.

I, Nephi, relate the prophecies of Isaiah which are recorded on the plates of brass: "Listen, children of Israel, who arise from the waters of Judah, which are the waters of baptism. You swear by the name of the Lord and talk about the God of Israel, but you do not do it in truth and righteousness, nor do you accept him. I have shown you the history of the early world and of your fathers and even events of the future, but you do not acknowledge or value them. But still for my name's sake, I will not become angry with you or cut you off. I have chosen you and refined you in the furnace of my affliction, for my word is eternal, and will be fulfilled. Listen, my children, for I am the first and the last. I created the world, and the stars and worlds of all creation. Who has declared these truths but the prophet?

AS foretold by Isaiah, the armies of Nebuchadnezzar besieged the city of Jerusalem.

JERUSALEM destroyed and the Jews being lead into bondage as Isaiah foretold.

The Lord loves him, and will honor him by fulfilling his prophecies. Babylon and the Chaldeans will be subject to his word.

"And I, Isaiah, have not given you these words in secret; so you have the opportunity to come near to me. If you had listened to the Lord's commandments, your peace would be like a river, your righteousness like the waves of the sea, and your children like the sands of the sea. So leave Babylon and the Chaldeans, and sing: 'The Lord hath redeemed his children. For he led them through the deserts and cleaved rocks from which water then flowed, so that they would not thirst. But even so, there is no peace for the wicked among you.'"

See Nephi 20:1-22

"EVEN though the house of Israel is dispersed, and even though families are broken off, driven away, and scattered abroad, they are still my people. Listen, those who live on the islands of the sea, those who live in distant lands! My voice is like a sharp sword or arrow. You are my servant, O Israel, in whom the Lord will be glorified, and both the tribes of Jacob and the Gentiles shall have the opportunity to come unto him.

"Then kings and princes shall see the Holy One of Israel and worship him, and no longer will he be despised. O islands of the sea, God shall give you his servants, the Messiah for a covenant of the people, to establish the earth, who will inherit the heritages that have been forgotten."

See 1 Nephi 21:1-8

"THEN you may say to exiles, 'Go forth!' And to those who sit in darkness, 'Come into the light!' And they shall not hunger or thirst, for the Lord will provide for them. Many will come from afar, from the north and west, and some from the land of Sinim. Sing, O heavens! Be joyful, O earth! For those in the east will have their heritage. Sing, O mountains! Peace be upon you, for the Lord has comforted his people. He cannot forget you, O house of Israel!"

See 1 Nephi 21:9-15

"LIFT up your eyes, O Israel! The families of the world gather together in the love they have for the Lord, and your enemies vanish. And Israel will be so numerous that the place of gathering will be enlarged to hold them, for no one will be lost. The Gentiles will help my children gather, and will even bring them to me in their arms and on their shoulders. Even kings and queens will look after my children. Those who have suffered the oppression of tyrants will be delivered to me, for the Lord will contend with their enemies and save them. All mankind will know the Lord, your Savior and Redeemer, the Mighty One of Jacob."

See 1 Nephi 21:16-26

AFTER I, Nephi, had read the prophecies of Isaiah to my brothers, they asked me what the prophecies meant. They asked whether the prophecies were only spiritual, and had nothing to do with the real world. But I said that they were given to Isaiah by the voice of the Spirit, in the way truths are made known to the prophets.

See 1 Nephi 22:1-2

I, Nephi, declared that the prophecies pertained to things both temporal and spiritual, that the house of Israel will be scattered over the earth, among all nations.

See 1 Nephi 22:3

I told my brothers that many are already lost from the knowledge of those in Jerusalem, that most of the tribes have been led away, even upon the islands of the sea, and that we do not know where they are.

See 1 Nephi 22:4

I said that the tribes are scattered and confounded and hated, because they hardened their hearts against the Lord. But the Gentiles would help them, literally, and would hold them up as a standard. After the scattering of the house of Israel, I told them the Lord will raise up a mighty nation among the Gentiles that will scatter our posterity.

See 1 Nephi 22:5-7

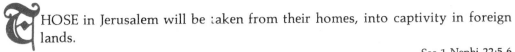

THOSE in Jerusalem will be taken from their homes, into captivity in foreign lands.

See 1 Nephi 22:5-6

AFTER the scattering of our children, the Lord will do a marvellous work among the Gentiles, which will help our children. It will be as if the Gentiles carried them in their arms and on their shoulders. And the work will be of great worth to the Gentiles themselves, and also to the whole house of Israel.

See 1 Nephi 22:7-9

COVENANTS between our Father in heaven and Abraham will be revealed—that in the seed of Abraham all the families of the earth will be blessed. And the earth will witness the redeeming power of God in Israel's behalf.

See 1 Nephi 22:10-11

THE Lord will bring the children of Israel out of captivity, and they will be gathered together in the lands of their inheritance. They will be brought out of darkness and obscurity into light, and they shall know that the Lord is their Savior and their Redeemer.

See 1 Nephi 22:12

BUT the blood of the false church will be poured upon them, and every nation will war against the children of Israel, and they will fall into the pit that will be dug to ensnare them. But all that fight against Zion will be destroyed, and the false church will tumble into dust.

See 1 Nephi 22:13-14

I, Nephi, told my brothers that the time will speedily come when Satan will have no more power over the children of men, when the proud and the wicked will be as stubble, ready to be burned. The anger of God shall be poured out soon on all the children of men because he will not let the wicked destroy the righteous.

See 1 Nephi 22:15-16

THE righteous of God will be saved by his power, even though the fullness of his anger comes and destroys their enemies by fire.

111

See 1 Nephi 22:17-19

THE Lord will prepare a way to fulfill the words of Moses: "The Lord will raise up to you a prophet like me, and those who do not listen to him will be cut off from among the people." This prophet is the Holy One of Israel, and he will judge righteously. But the righteous need not fear, for they will not be confounded.

112

See 1 Nephi 22:20-22

BUT I, Nephi, told my brothers that the kingdom of the devil would exist among the children of men, that all churches that are built to get gain, to get power over the flesh, to be popular in the world, to seek the lusts of the flesh, and to do all manner of iniquity belong to that kingdom. It is these churches that need to fear and tremble and quake, for they will tumble into the dust and will burn as stubble, according to the words of the prophet.

See 1 Nephi 22:23

THE time speedily comes when the righteous shall live happily under the Holy One of Israel. Then there shall be one voice and one shepherd, and Satan will have no power for a long time. And now I, Nephi, told my brothers that I wanted them to believe that the writings on the plates of brass are true, as many have testified, and that my brothers should obey God and endure to the end if they are to be saved at the last day. Amen.

See 1 Nephi 22:29-31

114

Pearls for Thought

by Alma E. Gygi

MAN DOES NOT WALK ALONE

The message within the few chapters illustrated in this volume is ages-old; indeed, it is the same message that God has always endeavored to impress upon His children—draw near to Me and I will draw near to you, whatever you desire in righteousness, asking with faith, and it shall be given you. History knows no occasion when the Lord forsook His children, but it is replete with examples of His children deserting Him. How would you act toward your children if you were God? How and on what basis would you bless them? To bless the unfaithful would do an injustice to the faithful, and God knowing this rewards with blessings or withholds them according to the worthiness of His children. The remarkable thing is that the Lord is always ready and willing to bless His children when they are ready to be blessed.

These chapters conclude with the final stages in the wilderness, the building of a ship under the Lord's direction, and the eventual crossing of the ocean and the landing of Lehi's group in the promised land. To help Lehi and his group accomplish this difficult task, the Lord supplied a remarkable instrument which not only gave them direction in their travels but information as to other necessities as well. The curious thing about this instrument was that it only worked according to the faith and the diligence of the group. Here again we see that while the Lord was willing to assist His children, He required something on their part in return. But even with all this assurance on the part of the Lord, it is not too surprising to see this group acting quite like human beings have always acted and continue to act. When everything is all right, man feels little need for the Lord, and when things go wrong, through man's own failure to abide by the requirements, he blames the Lord for it and accuses Him of withholding His blessings.

Few pages of history contain as much human drama as these, and certainly none give a more important lesson on how fortunate we are in being able to look back upon these pages and learn a lesson for ourselves. Notice the long-suffering and patience of the Lord. Each time (and the times are many) the offenders repented and turned from their rebelliousness, the Lord immediately kept good His promise and blessed them.

We are as much strangers in this land today as they were then; and we wander hopelessly in the dark if we do not take the hand of God. Life's "wilderness" today is just as troublesome and difficult to travel, but our paths become straight and our burdens light when we walk with the Lord. The promised land lies ahead—it is no mirage and it is to be possessed by the true and the faithful.

The Text of The Book of Mormon

THE FIRST BOOK OF NEPHI

HIS REIGN AND MINISTRY

CHAPTER 16.

7. And it came to pass that I, Nephi, took one of the daughters of Ishmael to wife; and also, my brethren took of the daughters of Ishmael to wife; and also Zoram took the eldest daughter of Ishmael to wife.

8. And thus my father had fulfilled all the commandments of the Lord which had been given unto him. And also, I, Nephi, had been blessed of the Lord exceedingly.

9. And it came to pass that the voice of the Lord spake unto my father by night, and commanded him that on the morrow he should take his journey into the wilderness.

10. And it came to pass that as my father arose in the morning, and went forth to the tent door, to his great astonishment he beheld upon the ground a round ball of curious workmanship; and it was of fine brass. And within the ball were two spindles; and the one pointed the way whither we should go into the wilderness.

11. And it came to pass that we did gather together whatsoever things we should carry into the wilderness, and all the remainder of our provisions which the Lord had given unto us; and we did take seed of every kind that we might carry into the wilderness.

12. And it came to pass that we did take our tents and depart into the wilderness, across the river Laman.

13. And it came to pass that we traveled for the space of four days, nearly a south-southeast direction, and we did pitch our tents again; and we did call the name of the place Shazer.

14. And it came to pass that we did take our bows and our arrows, and go forth into the wilderness to slay food for our families; and after we had slain food for our families we did return again to our families in the wilderness, to the place of Shazer. And we did go forth again in the wilderness, following the same direction, keeping in the most fertile parts of the wilderness, which were in the borders near the Red Sea.

15. And it came to pass that we did travel for the space of many days, slaying food by the way, with our bows and our arrows and our stones and our slings.

16. And we did follow the directions of the ball, which led us in the more fertile parts of the wilderness.

17. And after we had traveled for the space of many days, we did pitch our tents for the space of a time, that we might again rest ourselves and obtain food for our families.

18. And it came to pass that as I, Nephi, went forth to slay food, behold, I did break my bow, which was made of fine steel; and after I did break my bow, behold, my brethren were angry with me because of the loss of my bow, for we did obtain no food.

19. And it came to pass that we did return without food to our families, and being much fatigued, because of their journeying, they did suffer much for the want of food.

20. And it came to pass that Laman and Lemuel and the sons of Ishmael did begin to murmur exceedingly, because of their sufferings and afflictions in the wilderness; and also my father began to murmur against the Lord his God; yea, and they were all exceeding sorrowful, even that they did murmur against the Lord.

21. Now it came to pass that I, Nephi, having been afflicted with my brethren because of the loss of my bow, and their bows having lost their springs, it began to be exceedingly difficult, yea, insomuch that we could obtain no food.

22. And it came to pass that I, Nephi, did speak much unto my brethren, because they had hardened their hearts again, even unto complaining against the Lord their God.

23. And it came to pass that I, Nephi, did make out of wood a bow, and out of a straight stick, an arrow; wherefore, I did arm myself with a bow and an arrow, with a sling and with stones. And I said unto my father: Whither shall I go to obtain food?

24. And it came to pass that he did inquire of the Lord, for they had humbled themselves because of my word; for I did say many things unto them in the energy of my soul.

25. And it came to pass that the voice of the Lord came unto my father; and he was truly chastened because of his murmuring against the Lord, insomuch that he was brought down into the depths of sorrow.

26. And it came to pass that the voice of the Lord said unto him: Look upon the ball, and behold the things which are written.

27. And it came to pass that when my father beheld the things which were written upon the ball, he did fear and tremble exceedingly, and also my brethren and the sons of Ishmael and our wives.

28. And it came to pass that I, Nephi, beheld the pointers which were in the ball, that they did work according to the faith and diligence and heed which we did give unto them.

29. And there was also written upon them a new writing, which was plain to be read, which did give us understanding concerning the ways of the Lord; and it was written and changed from time to time, according to the faith and diligence which we gave unto it. And thus we see that by small means the Lord can bring about great things.

30. And it came to pass that I, Nephi, did go forth up into the top of the mountain, according to the directions which were given upon the ball.

31. And it came to pass that I did slay wild beasts, insomuch that I did obtain food for our families.

32. And it came to pass that I did return to our tents, bearing the beasts which I had slain; and now when they beheld that I had obtained food, how great was their joy! And it came to pass that they did humble themselves before the Lord, and did give thanks unto him.

33. And it came to pass that we did again take our journey, traveling nearly the same course as in the beginning; and after we had traveled for the space of many days we did pitch our tents again, that we might tarry for the space of a time.

34. And it came to pass that Ishmael died, and was buried in the place which was called Nahom.

35. And it came to pass that the daughters of Ishmael did mourn exceedingly, because of the loss of their father, and because of their afflictions in the wilderness; and they did murmur against my father, because he had brought them out of the land of Jerusalem, saying: Our father is dead; yea, and we have wandered much in the wilderness, and we have suffered much affliction, hunger, thirst, and fatigue; and after all these sufferings we must perish in the wilderness with hunger.

36. And thus they did murmur against my father, and also against me; and they were desirous to return again to Jerusalem.

37. And Laman said unto Lemuel and also unto the sons of Ishmael: Behold, let us slay our father, and also our brother Nephi, who has taken it upon him to be our ruler and our teacher, who are his elder brethren.

38. Now, he says that the Lord has talked with him, and also that angels have ministered unto him. But behold, we know that he lies unto us; and he tells us these things, and he worketh many things by his cunning arts, that he may deceive our eyes, thinking, perhaps, that he may lead us away into some strange wilderness; and after he has led us away, he has thought to make himself a king and a ruler over us, that he may do with us according to his will and pleasure. And after this manner did my brother Laman stir up their hearts to anger.

39. And it came to pass that the Lord was with us, yea, even the voice of the Lord came and did speak many words unto them, and did chasten them exceedingly; and after they were chastened by the voice of the Lord they did turn away their anger, and did repent of their sins, insomuch that the Lord did bless us again with food, that we did not perish.

CHAPTER 17.

1. And it came to pass that we did again take our journey in the wilderness; and we did travel nearly eastward from that time forth. And we did travel and wade through much affliction in the wilderness; and our women did bear children in the wilderness.

2. And so great were the blessings of the Lord upon us, that while we did live upon raw meat in the wilderness, our women did give plenty of suck for their children, and were strong, yea, even like unto the men; and they began to bear their journeyings without murmurings.

3. And thus we see that the commandments of God must be fulfilled. And if it so be that the children of men keep the commandments of God he doth nourish them, and strengthen them, and provide means whereby they can accomplish the thing which he has commanded them; wherefore, he did provide means for us while we did sojourn in the wilderness.

4. And we did sojourn for the space of many years, yea, even eight years in the wilderness.

5. And we did come to the land which we called Bountiful, because of its much fruit and also wild honey; and all these things were prepared of the Lord that we might not perish. And we beheld the sea, which we called Irreantum, which, being interpreted, is many waters.

6. And it came to pass that we did pitch our tents by the seashore; and notwithstanding we had suffered many afflictions and much difficulty, yea, even so much that we cannot write them all, we were exceedingly rejoiced when we came to the seashore; and we called the place Bountiful, because of its much fruit.

7. And it came to pass that after I, Nephi, had been in the land of Bountiful for the space of many days, the voice of the Lord came unto me, saying: Arise, and get thee into the mountain. And it came to pass that I arose and went up into the mountain, and cried unto the Lord.

8. And it came to pass that the Lord spake unto me, saying: Thou shalt construct a ship, after the manner which I shall show thee, that I may carry thy people across these waters.

9. And I said: Lord, whither shall I go that I may

find ore to molten, that I may make tools to construct the ship after the manner which thou hast shown unto me?

10.   And it came to pass that the Lord told me whither I should go to find ore, that I might make tools.

11.   And it came to pass that I, Nephi, did make a bellows wherewith to blow the fire, of the skins of beasts; and after I had made a bellows, that I might have wherewith to blow the fire, I did smite two stones together that I might make fire.

12.   For the Lord had not hitherto suffered that we should make much fire, as we journeyed in the wilderness; for he said: I will make thy food become sweet, that ye cook it not;

13.   And I will also be your light in the wilderness; and I will prepare the way before you, if it so be that ye shall keep my commandments; wherefore, inasmuch as ye shall keep my commandments ye shall be led towards the promised land; and ye shall know that it is by me that ye are led.

14.   Yea, and the Lord said also that: After ye have arrived in the promised land, ye shall know that I, the Lord, am God; and that I, the Lord, did deliver you from destruction; yea, that I did bring you out of the land of Jerusalem.

15.   Wherefore, I, Nephi, did strive to keep the commandments of the Lord, and I did exhort my brethren to faithfulness and diligence.

16.   And it came to pass that I did make tools of the ore which I did molten out of the rock.

17.   And when my brethren saw that I was about to build a ship, they began to murmur against me, saying: Our brother is a fool, for he thinketh that he can build a ship; yea, and he also thinketh that he can cross these great waters.

18.   And thus my brethren did complain against me, and were desirous that they might not labor, for they did not believe that I could build a ship; neither would they believe that I was instructed of the Lord.

19.   And now it came to pass that I, Nephi, was exceeding sorrowful because of the hardness of their hearts; and now when they saw that I began to be sorrowful they were glad in their hearts, insomuch that they did rejoice over me, saying: We knew that ye could not construct a ship, for we knew that ye were lacking in judgment; wherefore, thou canst not accomplish so great a work.

20.   And thou art like unto our father, led away by the foolish imaginations of his heart; yea, he hath led us out of the land of Jerusalem, and we have wandered in the wilderness for these many years; and our women have toiled, being big with child; and they have borne children in the wilderness and suffered all things, save it were death; and it would have been better that they had died before they came out of Jerusalem than to have suffered these afflictions.

21.   Behold, these many years we have suffered in the wilderness, which time we might have enjoyed our possessions and the land of our inheritance; yea, and we might have been happy.

22.   And we know that the people who were in the land of Jerusalem were a righteous people; for they kept the statutes and judgments of the Lord, and all his commandments, according to the law of Moses; wherefore, we know that they are a righteous people; and our father hath judged them, and hath led us away because we would hearken unto his words; yea, and our brother is like unto him. And after this manner of language did my brethren murmur and complain against us.

23.   And it came to pass that I, Nephi, spake unto them, saying: Do ye believe that our fathers, who were the children of Israel, would have been led away out of the hands of the Egyptians if they had not hearkened unto the words of the Lord?

24.   Yea, do ye suppose that they would have been led out of bondage, if the Lord had not commanded Moses that he should lead them out of bondage?

25.   Now ye know that the children of Israel were in bondage; and ye know that they were laden with tasks, which were grievous to be borne; wherefore, ye know that it must needs be a good thing for them, that they should be brought out of bondage.

26.   Now ye know that Moses was commanded of the Lord to do that great work; and ye know that by his word the waters of the Red Sea were divided hither and thither, and they passed through on dry ground.

27.   But ye know that the Egyptians were drowned in the Red Sea, who were the armies of Pharaoh.

28.   And ye also know that they were fed with manna in the wilderness.

29.   Yea, and ye also know that Moses, by his word according to the power of God which was in him, smote the rock, and there came forth water, that the children of Israel might quench their thirst.

30.   And notwithstanding they being led, the Lord their God, their Redeemer, going before them, leading them by day and giving light unto them by night, and doing all things for them which were expedient for man to receive, they hardened their hearts and blinded their minds, and reviled against Moses and against the true and living God.

31.   And it came to pass that according to his word he did destroy them; and according to his word he did lead them; and according to his word he did do all things for them; and there was not any thing done save it were by his word.

32.   And after they had crossed the river Jordan he did make them mighty unto the driving out of the children of the land, yea, unto the scattering them to destruction.

33.   And now, do ye suppose that the children of this

land, who were in the land of promise, who were driven out by our fathers, do ye suppose that they were righteous? Behold, I say unto you, Nay.

34. Do ye suppose that our fathers would have been more choice than they if they had been righteous? I say unto you, Nay.

35. Behold, the Lord esteemeth all flesh in one; he that is righteous is favored of God. But behold, this people had rejected every word of God, and they were ripe in iniquity; and the fulness of the wrath of God was upon them; and the Lord did curse the land against them, and bless it unto our fathers; yea, he did curse it against them unto their destruction, and he did bless it unto our fathers unto their obtaining power over it.

36. Behold, the Lord hath created the earth that it should be inhabited; and he hath created his children that they should possess it.

37. And he raiseth up a righteous nation, and destroyeth the nations of the wicked.

38. And he leadeth away the righteous into precious lands, and the wicked he destroyeth, and curseth the land unto them for their sakes.

39. He ruleth high in the heavens, for it is his throne, and this earth is his footstool.

40. And he loveth those who will have him to be their God. Behold, he loved our fathers, and he covenanted with them, yea, even Abraham, Isaac, and Jacob; and he remembered the covenants which he had made; wherefore, he did bring them out of the land of Egypt.

41. And he did straiten them in the wilderness with his rod; for they hardened their hearts, even as ye have; and the Lord straitened them because of their iniquity. He sent fiery flying serpents among them; and after they were bitten he prepared a way that they might be healed; and the labor which they had to perform was to look; and because of the simpleness of the way, or the easiness of it, there were many who perished.

42. And they did harden their hearts from time to time, and they did revile against Moses, and also against God; nevertheless, ye know that they were led forth by his matchless power into the land of promise.

43. And now, after all these things, the time has come that they have become wicked, yea, nearly unto ripeness; and I know not but they are at this day about to be destroyed; for I know that the day must surely come that they must be destroyed, save a few only, who shall be led away into captivity.

44. Wherefore, the Lord commanded my father that he should depart into the wilderness; and the Jews also sought to take away his life; yea, and ye also have sought to take away his life; wherefore, ye are murderers in your hearts and ye are like unto them.

45. Ye are swift to do iniquity but slow to remember the Lord your God. Ye have seen an angel, and he spake unto you; yea, ye have heard his voice from time to time; and he hath spoken unto you in a still small voice, but ye were past feeling, that ye could not feel his words; wherefore, he has spoken unto you like unto the voice of thunder, which did cause the earth to shake as if it were to divide asunder.

46. And ye also know that by the power of his almighty word he can cause the earth that it shall pass away; yea, and ye know that by his word he can cause the rough places to be made smooth, and smooth places shall be broken up. O, then, why is it, that ye can be so hard in your hearts?

47. Behold, my soul is rent with anguish because of you, and my heart is pained; I fear lest ye shall be cast off forever. Behold, I am full of the Spirit of God, insomuch that my frame has no strength.

48. And now it came to pass that when I had spoken these words, they were angry with me, and were desirous to throw me into the depths of the sea; and as they came forth to lay their hands upon me I spake unto them, saying: In the name of the Almighty God, I command you that ye touch me not, for I am filled with the power of God, even unto the consuming of my flesh; and whoso shall lay his hands upon me shall wither even as a dried reed; and he shall be as naught before the power of God, for God shall smite him.

49. And it came to pass that I, Nephi, said unto them that they should murmur no more against their father; neither should they withhold their labor from me, for God had commanded me that I should build a ship.

50. And I said unto them: If God had commanded me to do all things I could do them. If he should command me that I should say unto this water, be thou earth, it should be earth; and if I should say it, it would be done.

51. And now, if the Lord has such great power, and has wrought so many miracles among the children of men, how is it that he cannot instruct me, that I should build a ship?

52. And it came to pass that I, Nephi, said many things unto my brethren, insomuch that they were confounded and could not contend against me; neither durst they lay their hands upon me nor touch me with their fingers, even for the space of many days. Now they durst not do this lest they should wither before me, so powerful was the Spirit of God; and thus it had wrought upon them.

53. And it came to pass that the Lord said unto me: Stretch forth thine hand again unto thy brethren, and they shall not wither before thee, but I will shock them, saith the Lord, and this will I do, that they may know that I am the Lord their God.

54. And it came to pass that I stretched forth my hand unto my brethren, and they did not wither before me; but the Lord did shake them, even according to the word which he had spoken.

55. And now, they said: We know of a surety that the Lord is with thee, for we know that it is the power of the Lord that has shaken us. And they fell down before me, and were about to worship me, but I would not suffer them, saying: I am thy brother, yea, even thy younger brother; wherefore, worship the Lord thy God, and honor thy father and thy mother, that thy days may be long in the land which the Lord thy God shall give thee.

CHAPTER 18.

1. And it came to pass that they did worship the Lord, and did go forth with me; and we did work timbers of curious workmanship. And the Lord did show me from time to time after what manner I should work the timbers of the ship.

2. Now I, Nephi, did not work the timbers after the manner which was learned by men, neither did I build the ship after the manner of men; but I did build it after the manner which the Lord had shown unto me; wherefore, it was not after the manner of men.

3. And I, Nephi, did go into the mount oft, and I did pray oft unto the Lord; wherefore the Lord showed unto me great things.

4. And it came to pass that after I had finished the ship, according to the word of the Lord, my brethren beheld that it was good, and that the workmanship thereof was exceeding fine; wherefore, they did humble themselves again before the Lord.

5. And it came to pass that the voice of the Lord came unto my father, that we should arise and go down into the ship.

6. And it came to pass that on the morrow, after we had prepared all things, much fruits and meat from the wilderness, and honey in abundance, and provisions according to that which the Lord had commanded us, we did go down into the ship, with all our loading and our seeds, and whatsoever thing we had brought with us, every one according to his age; wherefore, we did all go down into the ship, with our wives and our children.

7. And now, my father had begat two sons in the wilderness; the elder was called Jacob and the younger Joseph.

8. And it came to pass after we had all gone down into the ship, and had taken with us our provisions and things which had been commanded us, we did put forth into the sea and were driven forth before the wind towards the promised land.

9. And after we had been driven forth before the wind for the space of many days, behold, my brethren and the sons of Ishmael and also their wives began to make themselves merry, insomuch that they began to dance, and to sing, and to speak with much rudeness, yea, even that they did forget by what power they had been brought thither; yea, they were lifted up unto exceeding rudeness.

10. And I, Nephi, began to fear exceedingly lest the Lord should be angry with us, and smite us because of our iniquity, that we should be swallowed up in the depths of the sea; wherefore, I, Nephi, began to speak to them with much soberness; but behold they were angry with me, saying: We will not that our younger brother shall be a ruler over us.

11. And it came to pass that Laman and Lemuel did take me and bind me with cords, and they did treat me with much harshness; nevertheless, the Lord did suffer it that he might show forth his power, unto the fulfilling of his word which he had spoken concerning the wicked.

12. And it came to pass that after they had bound me insomuch that I could not move, the compass, which had been prepared of the Lord, did cease to work.

13. Wherefore, they knew not whither they should steer the ship, insomuch that there arose a great storm, yea, a great and terrible tempest, and we were driven back upon the waters for the space of three days; and they began to be frightened exceedingly lest they should be drowned in the sea; nevertheless they did not loose me.

14. And on the fourth day, which we had been driven back, the tempest began to be exceeding sore.

15. And it came to pass that we were about to be swallowed up in the depths of the sea. And after we had been driven back upon the waters for the space of four days, my brethren began to see that the judgments of God were upon them, and that they must perish save that they should repent of their iniquities; wherefore, they came unto me, and loosed the bands which were upon my wrist, and behold they had swollen exceedingly; and also mine ankles were much swollen, and great was the soreness thereof.

16. Nevertheless, I did look unto my God, and I did praise him all the day long; and I did not murmur against the Lord because of mine afflictions.

17. Now my father, Lehi, had said many things unto them, and also unto the sons of Ishmael; but, behold, they did breathe out much threatenings against anyone that should speak for me; and my parents being stricken in years, and having suffered much grief because of their children, they were brought down, yea, even upon their sick-beds.

18. Because of their grief and much sorrow, and the iniquity of my brethren, they were brought near even to be carried out of this time to meet their God; yea, their grey hairs were about to be brought down to lie low in the dust;

yea, even they were near to be cast with sorrow into a watery grave.

19. And Jacob and Joseph also, being young, having need of much nourishment, were grieved because of the afflictions of their mother; and also my wife with her tears and prayers, and also my children, did not soften the hearts of my brethren that they would loose me.

20. And there was nothing save it were the power of God, which threatened them with destruction, could soften their hearts; wherefore, when they saw that they were about to be swallowed up in the depths of the sea they repented of the thing which they had done, insomuch that they loosed me.

21. And it came to pass after they had loosed me, behold, I took the compass, and it did work whither I desired it. And it came to pass that I prayed unto the Lord; and after I had prayed the winds did cease, and the storm did cease, and there was a great calm.

22. And it came to pass that I, Nephi, did guide the ship, that we sailed again towards the promised land.

23. And it came to pass that after we had sailed for the space of many days we did arrive at the promised land; and we went forth upon the land, and did pitch our tents; and we did call it the promised land.

24. And it came to pass that we did begin to till the earth, and we began to plant seeds; yea, we did put all our seeds into the earth, which we had brought from the land of Jerusalem. And it came to pass that they did grow exceedingly; wherefore, we were blessed in abundance.

25. And it came to pass that we did find upon the land of promise, as we journeyed in the wilderness, that there were beasts in the forests of every kind, both the cow and the ox, and the ass and the horse, and the goat and the wild goat, and all manner of wild animals, which were for the use of men. And we did find all manner of ore, both of gold, and of silver, and of copper.

CHAPTER 19.

1. And it came to pass that the Lord commanded me, wherefore I did make plates of ore that I might engraven upon them the record of my people. And upon the plates which I made I did engraven the record of my father, and also our journeyings in the wilderness, and the prophecies of my father; and also many of mine own prophecies have I engraven upon them.

2. And I knew not at the time when I made them that I should be commanded of the Lord to make these plates; wherefore, the record of my father, and the genealogy of his fathers, and the more part of all our proceedings in the wilderness are engraven upon those plates of which I have spoken; wherefore, the things which transpired before I made these plates are, of a truth, more particularly made

mention upon the first plates.

3. And after I had made these plates by way of commandment, I, Nephi, received a commandment that the ministry and the prophecies, the more plain and precious parts of them, should be written upon these plates; and that the things which were written should be kept for the instruction of my people, who should possess the land, and also for other wise purposes, which purposes are known unto the Lord.

4. Wherefore, I, Nephi, did make a record upon the other plates, which gives an account, or which gives a greater account of the wars and contentions and destructions of my people. And this have I done, and commanded my people what they should do after I was gone; and that these plates should be handed down from one generation to another, or from one prophet to another, until further commandments of the Lord.

5. And an account of my making these plates shall be given hereafter; and then, behold, I proceed according to that which I have spoken; and this I do that the more sacred things may be kept for the knowledge of my people.

6. Nevertheless, I do not write anything upon plates save it be that I think it be sacred. And now, if I do err, even did they err of old; not that I would excuse myself because of other men, but because of the weakness which is in me, according to the flesh, I would excuse myself.

7. For the things which some men esteem to be of great worth, both to the body and soul, others set at naught and trample under their feet. Yea, even the very God of Israel do men trample under their feet; I say, trample under their feet but I would speak in other words—they set him at naught, and hearken not to the voice of his counsels.

8. And behold he cometh, according to the words of the angel, in six hundred years from the time my father left Jerusalem.

9. And the world, because of their iniquity, shall judge him to be a thing of naught; wherefore they scourge him, and he suffereth it; and they smite him, and he suffereth it. Yea, they spit upon him, and he suffereth it, because of his loving kindness and his long-suffering towards the children of men.

10. And the God of our fathers, who were led out of Egypt, out of bondage, and also were preserved in the wilderness by him, yea, the God of Abraham, and of Isaac, and the God of Jacob, yieldeth himself, according to the words of the angel, as a man, into the hands of wicked men, to be lifted up, according to the words of Zenock, and to be crucified, according to the words of Neum, and to be buried in a sepulchre, according to the words of Zenos, which he spake concerning the three days of darkness, which should be a sign given of his death unto those who should inhabit the isles of the sea, more especially given unto those

who are of the house of Israel.

11. For thus spake the prophet: The Lord God surely shall visit all the house of Israel at that day, some with his voice, because of their righteousness, unto their great joy and salvation, and others with the thunderings and the lightnings of his power, by tempest, by fire, and by smoke, and vapor of darkness, and by the opening of the earth, and by mountains which shall be carried up.

12. And all these things must surely come, saith the prophet Zenos. And the rocks of the earth must rend; and because of the groanings of the earth, many of the kings of the isles of the sea shall be wrought upon by the Spirit of God, to exclaim: The God of nature suffers.

13. And as for those who are at Jerusalem, saith the prophet, they shall be scourged by all people, because they crucify the God of Israel, and turn their hearts aside, rejecting signs and wonders, and the power and glory of the God of Israel.

14. And because they turn their hearts aside, saith the prophet, and have despised the Holy One of Israel, they shall wander in the flesh, and perish, and become a hiss and a by-word, and be hated among all nations.

15. Nevertheless, when that day cometh, saith the prophet, that they no more turn aside their hearts against the Holy One of Israel, then will he remember the covenants which he made to their fathers.

16. Yea, then will he remember the isles of the sea; yea, and all the people who are of the house of Israel, will I gather in, saith the Lord, according to the words of the prophet Zenos, from the four quarters of the earth.

17. Yea, and all the earth shall see the salvation of the Lord, saith the prophet; every nation, kindred, tongue and people shall be blessed.

18. And I, Nephi, have written these things unto my people, that perhaps I might persuade them that they would remember the Lord their Redeemer.

19. Wherefore, I speak unto all the house of Israel, if it so be that they should obtain these things.

20. For behold, I have workings in the spirit, which doth weary me even that all my joints are weak, for those who are at Jerusalem; for had not the Lord been merciful, to show unto me concerning them, even as he had prophets of old, I should have perished also.

21. And he surely did show unto the prophets of old all things concerning them; and also he did show unto many concerning us; wherefore, it must needs be that we know concerning them for they are written upon the plates of brass.

22. Now it came to pass that I, Nephi, did teach my brethren these things; and it came to pass that I did read many things to them, which were engraven upon the plates of brass, that they might know concerning the doings of the Lord in other lands, among people of old.

23. And I did read many things unto them which were written in the book of Moses; but that I might more fully persuade them to believe in the Lord their Redeemer I did read unto them that which was written by the prophet Isaiah; for I did liken all scriptures unto us, that it might be for our profit and learning.

24. Wherefore I spake unto them, saying: Hear ye the words of the prophet, ye who are a remnant of the house of Israel, a branch who have been broken off; hear ye the words of the prophet, which were written unto all the house of Israel, and liken them unto yourselves, that ye may have hope as well as your brethren from whom ye have been broken off; for after this manner has the prophet written.

CHAPTER 20.

1. Hearken and hear this, O house of Jacob, who are called by the name of Israel, and are come forth out of the waters of Judah, or out of the waters of baptism, who swear by the name of the Lord, and make mention of the God of Israel, yet they swear not in truth nor in righteousness.

2. Nevertheless, they call themselves of the holy city, but they do not stay themselves upon the God of Israel, who is the Lord of Hosts; yea, the Lord of Hosts is his name.

3. Behold, I have declared the former things from the beginning; and they went forth out of my mouth, and I showed them. I did show them suddenly.

4. And I did it because I knew that thou art obstinate, and thy neck is an iron sinew, and thy brow brass;

5. And I have even from the beginning declared to thee; before it came to pass I showed them thee; and I showed them for fear lest thou shouldst say—Mine idol hath done them, and my graven image, and my molten image hath commanded them.

6. Thou hast seen and heard all this; and will ye not declare them? And that I have showed thee new things from this time, even hidden things, and thou didst not know them.

7. They are created now, and not from the beginning, even before the day when thou heardest them not they were declared unto thee, lest thou shouldst say—Behold I knew them.

8. Yea, and thou heardest not; yea, thou knewest not; yea, from that time thine ear was not opened; for I knew that thou wouldst deal very treacherously, and wast called a transgressor from the womb.

9. Nevertheless, for my name's sake will I defer mine anger, and for my praise will I refrain from thee, that I cut thee not off.

10. For, behold, I have refined thee, I have chosen thee in the furnace of affliction.

11. For mine own sake, yea, for mine own sake will I do this, for I will not suffer my name to be polluted, and I will not give my glory unto another.

12. Hearken unto me, O Jacob, and Israel my called, for I am he; I am the first, and I am also the last.

13. Mine hand hath also laid the foundation of the earth, and my right hand hath spanned the heavens. I call unto them and they stand up together.

14. All ye, assemble yourselves, and hear; who among them hath declared these things unto them? The Lord hath loved him; yea, and he will fulfill his word which he hath declared by them; and he will do his pleasure on Babylon, and his arm shall come upon the Chaldeans.

15. Also, saith the Lord; I the Lord, yea, I have spoken; yea, I have called him to declare, I have brought him, and he shall make his way prosperous.

16. Come ye near unto me; I have not spoken in secret; from the beginning, from the time that it was declared have I spoken; and the Lord God, and his Spirit, hath sent me.

17. And thus saith the Lord, thy Redeemer, the Holy One of Israel; I have sent him, the Lord thy God who teacheth thee to profit, who leadeth thee by the way thou shouldst go, hath done it.

18. O that thou hadst hearkened to my commandment—then had thy peace been as a river, and thy righteousness as the waves of the sea.

19. Thy seed also had been as the sand; the offspring of thy bowels like the gravel thereof; his name should not have been cut off nor destroyed from before me.

20. Go ye forth of Babylon, flee ye from the Chaldeans, with a voice of singing declare ye, tell this, utter to the end of the earth; say ye: The Lord hath redeemed his servant Jacob.

21. And they thirsted not; he led them through the deserts; he caused the waters to flow out of the rock for them; he clave the rock also and the waters gushed out.

22. And notwithstanding he hath done all this, and greater also, there is no peace, saith the Lord, unto the wicked.

CHAPTER 21.

1. And again: Hearken, O ye house of Israel, all ye that are broken off and are driven out, because of the wickedness of the pastors of my people; yea, all ye that are broken off, that are scattered abroad, who are of my people, O house of Israel. Listen, O isles, unto me, and hearken ye people from far; the Lord hath called me from the womb; from the bowels of my mother hath he made mention of my name.

2. And he hath made my mouth like a sharp sword; in the shadow of his hand hath he hid me, and made me a polished shaft; in his quiver he hid me;

3. And said unto me: Thou art my servant, O Israel, in whom I will be glorified.

4. Then I said, I have labored in vain, I have spent my strength for naught and in vain; surely my judgment is with the Lord, and my work with my God.

5. And now, saith the Lord—that formed me from the womb that I should be his servant, to bring Jacob again to him—though Israel be not gathered, yet shall I be glorious in the eyes of the Lord, and my God shall be my strength.

6. And he said: It is a light thing that thou shouldst be my servant to raise up the tribes of Jacob, and to restore the preserved of Israel. I will also give thee for a light to the Gentiles, that thou mayest be my salvation unto the ends of the earth.

7. Thus saith the Lord, the Redeemer of Israel, his Holy One, to him whom man despiseth, to him whom the nations abhorreth, to servant of rulers: Kings shall see and arise, princes also shall worship, because of the Lord that is faithful.

8. Thus saith the Lord: In an acceptable time have I heard thee, O isles of the sea, and in a day of salvation have I helped thee; and I will preserve thee, and give thee my servant for a covenant of the people, to establish the earth, to cause to inherit the desolate heritages;

9. That thou mayest say to the prisoners: Go forth; to them that sit in darkness: Show yourselves. They shall feed in the ways, and their pastures shall be in all high places.

10. They shall not hunger nor thirst, neither shall the heat nor the sun smite them; for he that hath mercy on them shall lead them, even by the springs of water shall he guide them.

11. And I will make all my mountains a way, and my highways shall be exalted.

12. And then, O house of Israel, behold, these shall come from far; and lo, these from the north and from the west; and these from the land of Sinim.

13. Sing, O heavens; and be joyful, O earth; for the feet of those who are in the east shall be established; and break forth into singing, O mountains; for they shall be smitten no more; for the Lord hath comforted his people, and will have mercy upon his afflicted.

14. But, behold, Zion hath said: The Lord hath forsaken me, and my Lord hath forgotten me—but he will show that he hath not.

15. For can a woman forget her sucking child, that she should not have compassion on the son of her womb? Yea, they may forget, yet will I not forget thee, O house of Israel.

16. Behold, I have graven thee upon the palms of my hands; thy walls are continually before me.

17. Thy children shall make haste against thy destroyers; and they that made thee waste shall go forth of thee.

18. Lift up thine eyes round about and behold; all these gather themselves together, and they shall come to thee. And as I live, saith the Lord, thou shalt surely clothe thee with them all, as with an ornament, and bind them on even as a bride.

19. For thy waste and thy desolate places, and the land of thy destruction, shall even now be too narrow by reason of the inhabitants; and they that swallowed thee up shall be far away.

20. The children whom thou shalt have, after thou hast lost the first, shall again in thine ears say: The place is too strait for me; give place to me that I may dwell.

21. Then shalt thou say in thine heart: Who hath begotten me these, seeing I have lost my children, and am desolate, a captive, and removing to and fro? And who hath brought up these? Behold, I was left alone; these, where have they been?

22. Thus saith the Lord God: Behold, I will lift up mine hand to the Gentiles, and set up my standard to the people; and they shall bring thy sons in their arms, and thy daughters shall be carried upon their shoulders.

23. And kings shall be thy nursing fathers, and their queens thy nursing mothers; they shall bow down to thee with their face towards the earth, and lick up the dust of thy feet; and thou shalt know that I am the Lord; for they shall not be ashamed that wait for me.

24. For shall the prey be taken from the mighty, or the lawful captives delivered?

25. But thus saith the Lord, even the captives of the mighty shall be taken away, and the prey of the terrible shall be delivered; for I will contend with him that contendeth with thee, and I will save thy children.

26. And I will feed them that oppress thee with their own flesh; they shall be drunken with their own blood as with sweet wine; and all flesh shall know that I, the Lord, am thy Savior and thy Redeemer, the Mighty One of Jacob.

CHAPTER 22.

1. And now it came to pass that after I, Nephi, had read these things which were engraven upon the plates of brass, my brethren came unto me and said unto me: What meaneth these things which ye have read? Behold, are they to be understood according to things which are spiritual, which shall come to pass according to the spirit and not the flesh?

2. And I, Nephi, said unto them: Behold they were manifest unto the prophet by the voice of the Spirit; for by the Spirit are all things made known unto the prophets, which shall come upon the children of men according to the flesh.

3. Wherefore, the things of which I have read are things pertaining to things both temporal and spiritual; for it appears that the house of Israel, sooner or later, will be scattered upon all the face of the earth, and also among all nations.

4. And behold, there are many who are already lost from the knowledge of those who are at Jerusalem. Yea, the more part of all the tribes have been led away; and they are scattered to and fro upon the isles of the sea; and whither they are none of us knoweth, save that we know that they have been led away.

5. And since they have been led away, these things have been prophesied concerning them, and also concerning all those who shall hereafter be scattered and be confounded, because of the Holy One of Israel; for against him will they harden their hearts; wherefore, they shall be scattered among all nations and shall be hated of all men.

6. Nevertheless, after they shall be nursed by the Gentiles, and the Lord has lifted up his hand upon the Gentiles and set them up for a standard, and their children have been carried in their arms, and their daughters have been carried upon their shoulders, behold these things of which are spoken are temporal; for thus are the covenants of the Lord with our fathers; and it meaneth us in the days to come, and also all our brethren who are of the house of Israel.

7. And it meaneth that the time cometh that after all the house of Israel have been scattered and confounded, that the Lord God will raise up a mighty nation among the Gentiles, yea, even upon the face of this land; and by them shall our seed be scattered.

8. And after our seed is scattered the Lord God will proceed to do a marvelous work among the Gentiles, which shall be of great worth unto our seed; therefore, it is likened unto their being nourished by the Gentiles and being carried in their arms and upon their shoulders.

9. And it shall also be of worth unto the Gentiles; and not only unto the Gentiles but unto all the house of Israel, unto the making known of the covenants of the Father of heaven unto Abraham, saying: In thy seed shall all the kindreds of the earth be blessed.

10. And I would, my brethren, that ye should know that all the kindreds of the earth cannot be blessed unless he shall make bare his arm in the eyes of the nations.

11. Wherefore, the Lord God will proceed to make bare his arm in the eyes of all the nations, in bringing about his covenants and his gospel unto those who are of the house of Israel.

12. Wherefore, he will bring them again out of captivity, and they shall be gathered together to the lands of their inheritance; and they shall be brought out of obscurity and out of darkness; and they shall know that the Lord is their Savior and their Redeemer, the Mighty One of Israel.

13. And the blood of that great and abominable church, which is the whore of all the earth, shall turn upon their own heads; for they shall war among themselves, and the sword of their own hands shall fall upon their own heads, and they shall be drunken with their own blood.

14. And every nation which shall war against thee, O house of Israel, shall be turned one against another, and they shall fall into the pit which they digged to ensnare the people of the Lord. And all that fight against Zion shall be destroyed, and that great whore, who hath perverted the right ways of the Lord, yea, that great and abominable church, shall tumble to the dust and great shall be the fall of it.

15. For behold, saith the prophet, the time cometh speedily that Satan shall have no more power over the hearts of the children of men; for the day soon cometh that all the proud and they who do wickedly shall be as stubble; and the day cometh that they must be burned.

16. For the time soon cometh that the fulness of the wrath of God shall be poured out upon all the children of men; for he will not suffer that the wicked shall destroy the righteous.

17. Wherefore, he will preserve the righteous by his power, even if it so be that the fulness of his wrath must come, and the righteous be preserved, even unto the destruction of their enemies by fire. Wherefore, the righteous need not fear; for thus saith the prophet, they shall be saved, even if it so be as by fire.

18. Behold, my brethren, I say unto you, that these things must shortly come; yea, even blood, and fire, and vapor of smoke must come; and it must needs be upon the face of this earth; and it cometh unto men according to the flesh if it so be that they will harden their hearts against the Holy One of Israel.

19. For behold, the righteous shall not perish; for the time surely must come that all they who fight against Zion shall be cut off.

20. And the Lord will surely prepare a way for his people, unto the fulfilling of the words of Moses, which he spake, saying: A prophet shall the Lord your God raise up unto you, like unto me; him shall ye hear in all things whatsoever he shall say unto you. And it shall come to pass that all those who will not hear that prophet shall be cut off from among the people.

21. And now I, Nephi, declare unto you, that this prophet of whom Moses spake was the Holy One of Israel; wherefore, he shall execute judgment in righteousness.

22. And the righteous need not fear, for they are those who shall not be confounded. But it is the kingdom of the devil, which shall be built up among the children of men, which kingdom is established among them which are in the flesh—

23. For the time speedily shall come that all churches which are built up to get gain, and all those who are built up to get power over the flesh, and those who are built up to become popular in the eyes of the world, and those who seek the lusts of the flesh and the things of the world, and to do all manner of iniquity; yea, in fine, all those who belong to the kingdom of the devil are they who need fear, and tremble, and quake; they are those who must be brought low in the dust; they are those who must be consumed as stubble; and this is according to the words of the prophet.

24. And the time cometh speedily that the righteous must be led up as calves of the stall, and the Holy One of Israel must reign in dominion, and might, and power, and great glory.

25. And he gathereth his children from the four quarters of the earth; and he numbereth his sheep, and they know him; and there shall be one fold and one shepherd; and he shall feed his sheep, and in him they shall find pasture.

26. And because of the righteousness of his people, Satan has no power; wherefore, he cannot be loosed for the space of many years; for he hath no power over the hearts of the people, for they dwell in righteousness, and the Holy One of Israel reigneth.

27. And now behold, I, Nephi, say unto you that all these things must come according to the flesh.

28. But, behold, all nations, kindreds, tongues, and people shall dwell safely in the Holy One of Israel if it so be that they will repent.

29. And now I, Nephi, make an end; for I durst not speak further as yet concerning these things.

30. Wherefore, my brethren, I would that ye should consider that the things which have been written upon the plates of brass are true; and they testify that a man must be obedient to the commandments of God.

31. Wherefore, ye need not suppose that I and my father are the only ones that have testified, and also taught them. Wherefore, if ye shall be obedient to the commandments, and endure to the end, ye shall be saved at the last day. And thus it is. Amen.

"Moroni's Challenge"

And when ye shall receive these things, I would exhort you that ye would ask God, the Eternal Father, in the name of Christ, if these things are not true; and if ye shall ask with a sincere heart, with real intent, having faith in Christ, he will manifest the truth of it unto you, by the power of the Holy Ghost. Moroni 10:4.

E wish to express our deep appreciation to The First Presidency of The Church of Jesus Christ of Latter-day Saints for their allowing us to use, in this publication, the text of the Book of Mormon. We print here only the text for that part covered by the illustrations. Subsequent volumes will contain the text for the parts each volume covers.

We do not print here any other material found in various copyrighted editions of the Book of Mormon, such as the prefatory material and other writings found prior to the First Book of Nephi.

— The Publishers

PREVIEW OF VOLUME IV

Volume IV of *Illustrated Stories from the Book of Mormon* will be as exciting and beautiful as the three previous publications of this work.

You will be anxious to see the portrayal of the writings of Isaiah as recorded on the Brass Plates. Nephi taught his people from these writings. Many of these prophetic recordings have much to do with our day as well as applying to Nephi's people and their descendants.

Volume IV will be available in the very near future and will cover that portion of the Book of Mormon known as the Second Book of Nephi.